Bureaucracy
and
Technocracy
in the
Socialist
Countries

Bureaucracy and Technocracy in the Socialist Countries

SERGE MALLET

Spokesman Books

1974

European Socialist Thought: No. 1

Published by the Bertrand Russell Peace Foundation
for *Spokesman Books*, Bertrand Russell House,
Gamble Street, Nottingham NG7 4ET

© Spokesman Books 1974
ISBN 0 85124 086 0

Printed by the Russell Press Ltd., Gamble Street,
Nottingham (TU)

Contents

Series Introduction   **VII**

Foreword   **IX**

I   Ideals and Reality in the Socialist
Countries   **11**

II   Bureaucratic States in Eastern Europe   **20**

III   A New Working Class   **25**

IV   "Reform": Retrospect and Prospects   **40**

V   After the Soviet Intervention in
Czechoslovakia   **59**

Series Introduction

Having passed through a veritable Dark Age, in which dogmatism and obscurantism held a world-wide predominance, and flourished alongside small-minded provinciality, socialist thought has, during the past two decades, undergone a veritable renaissance, affecting almost every major European country, East or West. The collapse of Stalinist orthodoxy has been accompanied by a renewal of radical thinking in some of the older social-democratic and communist parties, and the growth of several independent schools of young intellectuals who have been profoundly influenced by ideals of socialist humanism.

Unfortunately, much of the most audacious and relevant thinking in France, Italy, Hungary, Yugoslavia, Belgium and Germany has been kept out of reach in Britain by a combination of difficulties: commercial publishers have been conservative in taking on commitments unless the authors in question have been glamorous, publicity-attractive figures; all those works which have had a strong empirical base in the experience of a national labour movement have tended to escape translation because it is widely assumed that the English-speaking public is not interested in the detailed sociology of other European countries; and the specialist socialist publishing houses have been highly selective in their choice of doctrinal filters for a variety of reasons.

Extracts from the writings of such men as Mallet, Marković or Goldmann have been featured in the periodical press in Britain, and some of the specialist works of these authors have found respectable imprints. But not only have major works escaped translation: so too have numerous practical, polemical and agitational writings, some of which are of very great interest to all socialists.

The object of this series is to begin to remedy some of these deficiencies. It is hoped to make available a number of important original works of analysis as well as some more directly propagandist essays which will assist the Labour Movements of the English-speaking world to understand their colleagues. But it is also hoped that the series may assist in widening the dialogue between socialists in East and West Europe, and emphasising the organic unity of their interests and concerns.

Ken Coates, 1974.

Foreword

The main part of this book, which forms its first four chapters, developed out of two speeches presented by the author in the late 'sixties. The first was delivered to the Korcula Summer School in Dalmatia, where since 1963 Marxist philosophers and sociologists from the East and the West have held annual meetings, and the second at the Colloquium in Herzegovina (Montenegro) organised by the Institute for Social Sciences in Belgrade and the Gramsci Institute in Rome, at which sociologists from all the Eastern countries (including the USSR) discussed "Social Stratification in Socialist Countries".

The author himself wrote a short introduction to the text, which reads:

"The last part of the article, 'The Technocratic-Bureaucratic Antagonism and the Imperial Contest,' was written later, in July 1968, after the advent of the 'Czechoslovakian Spring'. Subsequent events in Czechoslovakia do not make necessary any revision of the article. If it did not predict them, it nevertheless analysed the context in which they occurred. That context is one of the dual conflict within the socialist countries: a conflict for power between the bureaucratic class and the new technological elites of 'Soviet' society, and between the 'imperial consciousness" of the Soviet Union and the desire for a self-managed socialism on the part of the new intellectual, technical, and industrial working classes of the European People's Democracies. The recourse to armed intervention, taking into account the risk to the cohesion of the 'world socialist camp' and to peace itself, signified that the dual conflict analysed in these pages had reached a point of contradiction where 'the ammunition of critical exchange is ready to give way to a critical exchange of ammunition.'

As socialists, we may be saddened that the resolution of internal contradictions in the socialist camp is accomplished by resort to brutal military force. But, as Marxists, we shouldn't be too surprised. If it is true that force is the midwife of social revolution, the passage of Eastern countries from the primitive stage of state capitalism to that of realised socialism can scarcely be imagined without a long, painful process of prolonged struggles and sharp conflicts. In the end, the most important thing is not this or that episode in the historical struggle, but that the masses of the 'socialist' countries rediscover political struggle and that the desire for socialism, contrary to what happened in Hungary in 1956, no longer be discouraged, but rather affirmed with a new vigour.

The author of this article has been convinced for many years that there is no society in existence that is truly socialist. The 'socialism' of the Eastern countries, even in its liberal version, is to socialism what the monsters of the paleolithic era are to present animal species: clumsy, abortive, prototypes."

These speeches of Mallet were originally translated for the American Journal *Socialist Revolution* and we would like to thank them for allowing us to use their translation as the basis for our own text.

The final chapter was originally given as a paper at the Bertrand Russell Peace Foundation's Conference on Czechoslovakia in Stockholm, February 1969.

Ken Fleet

X

1

Ideals and Reality in the Socialist Countries

Self-Management and Socialism

The concept of self-management cannot be studied abstractly in terms of an ideal and timeless society. The degree to which economic and social self-management is practised is one of the most significant indices of the level in the development of the new social relations among human beings that socialism seeks to achieve. Yet fifty years' experience in states that claim to be socialist shows the extent to which the concept of a socialist society can be altered and modified to match the level of productive forces attained in a country where a political revolution has occurred. A political revolution can modify the character of the ownership of the means of production, but it is not sufficient for modifying the nature of social relations. In order that management, not only of the means of production and exchange, but also of the society as a whole, cease to be the domain of a minority felt as oppresive by the majority, the political revolution must be accompanied by an equally profound social revolution, one in which the relations of "the governed" give way to relations of egalitarian co-operation. The development of self-management as a substitute for administrative management does not result in a particular form of socialism, but is an absolute imperative for a socialist society.

Of course, there can be specific national or historical forms of self-management. But there can be no socialism without self-management — in the larger sense of social self-management and not in the narrow sense of the management of autonomous units of production.

Fifty years after the October Revolution, twenty years after the passage to socialism in Eastern Europe, fifteen years after the success of the Chinese revolution, the development of worker and social self-management remains embryonic in all socialist countries. Even in the Federated People's Republic of Yugoslavia, the only country that made self-management its fundamental social principle, its realization seems to be undergoing retardation rather than advance.

The Marxist masters had thought the transition from political to social revolution would be very short, because for them the "withering away of the state" was to begin the very day that the working class seized political power. But today, the concepts of bureaucracy and technocracy, concepts developed by Western sociologists outside the context of Marxist analysis, are accepted as operational concepts by Marxist sociologists of the socialist countries in order to analyze their own society.

Most of our colleagues in Eastern Europe analyze even the process of economic reform now taking place in all Eastern European countries as the product of a conflict between the state bureaucratic class that presided over the development of heavy industry during a period of authoritarian planning and a new class of economic directors who are fighting for the economic and social flexibility appropriate to industrial diversification and who want to create a large class of consumers capable of influencing the quality and orientation of socialist production.

Technocratic-Bureaucratic Conflict in the Socialist Countries

The sociologists of The Institute of Social Sciences in Budapest have proposed the newest and most challenging conception of this conflict in the socialist countries. They see the development of socialism taking place by means of an alliance of advanced socialists and the technocracy against the archaic bureaucracy, which has slowed down the historial development of the socialist countries and has kept them in an outmoded phase of development in which the bureaucracy's political monopoly will be secure. The passage of economic-political power from the bureaucratic stratum to the technocratic stratum would represent an essential element in the passage from one phase to another in the development of socialism.

But how can the appearance of a bureaucratic or technocratic stratum be integrated into the concept of a socialist society? Bureaucratic and technocratic strata have no place in a fully socialist society — even if they constitute necessary phases in its development. What, then, are the social and organizational forces at the heart of those countries with a socialist structure that will assure passage to more democratic forms of social management? Such a passage is an indispensable condition for the abolition of exploitation and the liberation of collective and individual creativity.

The answer to these various questions can only be sketched here, especially since the necessary materials for such an analysis are still not at our disposal. The explosive development of the social sciences in the socialist countries indicates that we will be able to see the deeper nature of these societies more clearly a few years from now, and perhaps to elucidate in a more realistic fashion the complex relations of their economic infrastructure, social structures and political superstructures. But we can begin to make some observations now in the light of the loosening of bureaucratic constraints that has taken place in Eastern Europe since the days of Stalin.

The Formation of the Bureaucracy in Socialist Countries

Socialist political regimes in Eastern Europe all came about under socio-historical conditions different from those foreseen by Marx. In some countries, the Marxist-Leninist wing of the workers' movement found itself in the leadership of democratic movements that did not initially have socialist objectives. In Russia and China, the political revolution occurred in the frame-work of an agrarian revolution for land and peace. In Yugoslavia, it was the expression of a movement for unification and national liberation. In the other Eastern European countries, it was exported into the country as a consequence of the Red Army's military victories and the refusal of traditional

Figure representing a bureaucrat is overrun by
"expertise."
From Tukor (Budapest), Oct. 17, 1967.

political forces to collaborate with it. Whatever the case, the political revolutions were never principally the product of a revolutionary class, which in these countries was still too small to constitute a decisive political force. (Only Czechoslovakia was a relatively developed industrial nation, but the 1947 revolution, effected for reasons of the USSR's international strategy and initially against the will of the Czech Communists, deviated from the historical process that was in course since 1945.)

The Formation of Bureaucratic States from the 17th to 19th Centuries

In all socialist countries, the seizure of political power by the workers' movement (under Communist direction or by the Communists alone, according to the case) occurred within the framework of a particular historical situation which Western Europe had experienced between the seventeenth and nineteenth centuries. The framework was one of a proto-capitalist phase of development. It was characterized by the advanced formation of bureaucratic centralized states, which made possible the establishment of the first capital reserves, the primitive accumulation of capital forced on the back of the peasantry and a fraction of the old pre-capitalist middle classes, and the creation of a capitalist market extended to the whole population.

Victorian England, Napoleonic France and the Germany of Bismarck constitute examples of this phase, whereas the Czarist and Austro-Hungarian empires had just entered it in the beginning of the twentieth century. Beginning with the formation of finance capital as a fusion of banking and industrial capital, the forms of the bureaucratic state entered into conflict with the development of the productive forces and inhibited the formation of the financial market and the initiative of the free market. The Russian revolution appeared as a brutal rupture in the process that had had a much slower evolution in Western Europe.

Liberal Capitalism and the Bureaucratic State

The Bolsheviks were confronted with the need to raise the level of development of the whole of the backward Czarist empire to that attained by the industrialized regions of Russia where the revolutionary movement had crystallized. The Bolsheviks, contrary to the profoundest thoughts of Marx and Engels, did not move to destroy the bureaucratic Czarist state. On the contrary, they used its structures to make possible a gigantic leap in industrial production. But that leap was limited precisely to those sectors of the base (steel production, energy production) that in the nineteenth century West were under the control of the bureaucratic state rather than private capital.

The Formation of Stalinist Bureaucracy

Stalinist Bureaucracy, as a ruling caste, is the historical product of the leap beyond and over the phase of liberal capitalism. In addition, its formation appears as an amalgamation of the old "urban revolutionary" class, transplanted after several years of partisan struggles into the backward conditions of the Russian countryside, and the old Czarist provincial bureaucracy, which had rallied to the new regime all the while retaining the essence of its old habits.

In the resulting bureaucratic detour taken by the new regime, one cannot be certain that these latter "leftovers from the past" weighed more heavily than the neophytes. (The publication of the Archives of the Party Committee of the town and region of Smolensk casts a harsh light on the struggles that the central power had to wage against former revolutionaries turned Oriental satraps.)

In 1922, Lenin, in his testament, unequivocally expressed his fears about the rise of this new bureaucratic class. He feared that it would become a new ground for something he detested very much — Russian national chauvinism: "We call ours an apparatus that in fact is still basically foreign to us and represents a hash of bourgeois and Czarist holdovers, which were absolutely impossible for us to transform in five years because we lacked the help of other countries, and because we were pre-occupied militarily and were also fighting famine."

"In these conditions, it is completely natural that the 'freedom to leave the union,' which seemed to us a sufficient statement of policy, should appear in fact as a bureaucratic formula incapable of defending the people of other races in the USSR against the invasion of the authentic Russian, the nationalistic Russian, the chauvinist, the idiot, and the oppressor, which is what the typical Russian bureaucrat basically is. Nor can it be doubted that the Soviet and sovietized workers, who are a small minority, will also drown themselves, like flies in a bowl of milk, in this ocean of Russian national rabble . . . .

"Have we taken careful enough measures really to defend the Soviet peoples of other races against

18

the typical Russian slavedriver? I think that we have not taken these measures, and that it was really incumbent upon us to have done so and to do so." (December 30, letter to the Central Committee.)

The total nationalization of economic activity that this class directed through the state apparatus gave it, in the absence of any opposition from the workers, an economic base of power quite superior to that of the old Czarist bureaucracy. The basis of this power was a still archaic undifferentiated heavy industry, which by its nature was susceptible to non-economic control. (From the same point of view, one must understand the apparent failure of the collective farm [*kolkoz*] system. Its essential object was less to give a socialist structure to the peasantry than to impose upon it a framework of production which, as in the old mode of Asiatic production, would allow a rigorous tax assessment destined to assure both the development of heavy industry and the maintenance of the bureaucratic stratum.)

2

Bureaucratic States in Eastern Europe

In the European states detached from the Czarist or old Austro-Hungarian empires, as in the Balkan countries recently liberated from the Ottoman empire, a national bourgeoisie arose too late to control primary economic development; foreign imperialist capital had already conquered the most important positions. Political power, in Hungary as in Poland, in Rumania as in Yugoslavia, took the form of an unstable equilibrium between the old bureaucracy and still strong feudal elements.

The Bureaucratic States in Central and Eastern Europe

Nowhere, not even in Czechoslovakia, did the national bourgeoisie find itself strong enough to create liberal democratic political structures or a semi-independent capitalist economy. The political revolution took place between 1945 and 1950 under the direction of Communist cells, which had little real influence in the country and could do little to modify the position of the bureaucracy. The very weakness of the working class and of its militant core, which had gone through twenty-five years of uninterrupted fascist repression, favoured the creation of a bureaucratic stratum, a stratum formed in part from elements of the old bureaucracy which had allied with the regime and in part from new notables of peasant origin. In most of the People's Democracies, with the exception of Czechoslovakia and Yugoslavia, the revolutionary elements that arose from within the intelligentsia and the working class constituted from the beginning only a small group of militants. The purges of the 1947—1953 era were to reduce them still further. As a result, the process of penetration into the Party of a bureaucratic stratum of *"parvenus of the revolution"* was even more extensive and rapid than in the Soviet Union.

Thus, the roots of the bureaucratization of the socialist state in both Stalinist Russia and in the People's Democracies between 1947 and 1955 go back to the bureaucratic structures of regimes that predated the October Revolution and the establishment of the People's Democratic states. But it would be misleading to draw a straight line from the bureaucracy of the old regime to the new bureaucracy. The Czarist bureaucracy (and the various national bureaucratic classes that came into power in the Balkans and Central Europe after the break-up of the Austro-Hungarian, Czarist and Ottoman empires) had to share its power with still powerful feudal classes, and thus had to seek the aid of foreign capital in order to organize industrial development. The assumption of power by the Communist parties ended the power both of the feudal classes and of foreign capital.

The new bureaucracy, heir to the traditions and often the personnel of the old one, was nevertheless able to achieve, although with difficulty, a primitive accumulation of capital. Whereas the

21

Western bureaucracies had achieved this for their bourgeoisies toward the middle of the nineteenth century, the Eastern countries, economically backward in comparison to their Western competitors, had little success in doing so. We must thus recognize the positive character of the bureaucratic phase through which all the socialist countries passed. This explains the popularity that the bureaucracy enjoyed, despite its police methods and its despotism. The resistance of the Soviet people to Nazi aggression was the surest measure of this.

The Historical Function of the Bureaucracy

The October Revolution notwithstanding its socialist aspirations, and the political revolutions that occurred in Eastern and Central Europe after 1945, allowed the bureaucratic stratum, as a social expression of primitive state capitalism, to play an historic role in the passage of agrarian societies to the primary phase of industrial society. It was a passage that these countries, because of their "historical lag", could not achieve in the framework of traditional capitalist structures.

This interpretation of the historical development of the socialist countries supports Lenin against Kautsky, when he asserted that because of the imperialist character of the states first entering the capitalist era, the automatic passage from feudalism to capitalism had become impossible for most backward countries. But this interpretation also supports Kautsky against Lenin, when the Austro-Marxist argued that because of the insufficient development of its productive forces, the direct passage to socialism was impossible in Czarist Russia.

What conclusions can we now draw from this interpretation? 1) The first phase of socialism — what Marx and Engels as well as Lenin called the "dictatorship of the proletariat" — implies the withering away of the state beginning as soon as power is seized. Insofar as the bureaucratic phase in socialist countries implies the continuation of the exploitation of man by man (which need not be tied to the particular process of capital accumulation, only one of the diverse forms it has assumed) this bureaucratic phase should not be confused with the "first phase of socialism".

Socialism or Society in Transition

Although certain conditions indispensible to the realization of socialism, especially the nationalization of the principal means of production and exchange, have been realized, others equally important, such as the democratisation of economic management and of the state apparatus, were not set in motion during this period. We are thus led to speak of a society in transition towards socialism and not of a socialist society. This historical revision of vocabulary would have extraordinarily positive consequences for the revitalisation of the concept of socialism in Western European countries. 2) Just as discussions now in progress on the question of "the Asiatic mode of production" make it appear that humanity had two different models for the dissolution of primitive community, namely the ancient (or slave) mode of production and the Asiatic mode of production, so we can accept the hypothesis that the capitalist mode of production was the West's own way of passing from agrarian civilization to industrial society. The fact that it arrived first in

Western Europe and the United States is precisely the reason why other societies were prevented from taking that path. At the same time, the arrival of capitalism in Western Europe engendered the diffusion of Western life style, models and products that everywhere sapped the base of the ancient agrarian societies, just as the imperialist development of the Greek and Roman slave societies doubtless counteracted tendencies in this direction within Eastern Mediterranean societies. 3) The revolutions of the Eastern countries and Central Europe — the first and most powerfully affected by this diffusion — found the framework for non-capitalist and non-imperialist development in the pre-existing structures of the bureaucratic state. The socialist revolutions in some ways liberated the productive tendencies of the state bureaucracy, tendencies which couldn't develop in the West because of the growth of finance capital and the political weight of the middle class, but which existed embryonically in the beginning of the capitalist era and permitted its development. 4) Whatever feelings of sadness it causes us, history — since October, 1917 — was neither with the anarchist peasants of Makhno, nor with the sailors and workers of the libertarian commune of Kronstadt; instead it was firmly with the Bolshevik centralisers who, from Trotsky when he was in power, to Stalin, created the conditions for the liberation of the productive forces by giving power to bureaucracy. The Russian people, as Gorky's hero Thomas Gordeiev expressed so well, did not reproach the Czarist bureaucracy for its very existence as a bureaucracy, but rather for its impotence in assuming effectively its historical task.

3

A New Working Class

The Appropriation of Surplus Value by the State: The Foundation of Bureaucratic Power

There exist thousands of definitions of "bureaucracy" — from that of Stalin, of whom Trotsky said that "when he spoke of it (and he spoke of it often), he had in mind only the bad habits of bureau employees," to that of Bruno Rizzi, who gives it the characteristics of an autonomous class. In fact, however, there is only one definition, crude as it is, that encompasses all bureaucratic situations: bureaucracy is, above all, the reign of the tax collector, the treasury, to whom a social group, large or small, delegates the power to appropriate, through civilian or military constraint, the surplus value created by the work of the state's subjects. The policeman, the judge, and the soldier are in the last analysis only the secular arm of the treasury. When the level of the productive forces and the level of demographic growth are more or less in equilibrium and the maintenance of the ruling classes, including the bureaucracy itself, can be handled by an appropriation which the populace finds supportable, then the weight of the bureaucracy in the society is weak and its autonomous power insignificant. When, on the contrary, the level of production is insufficient to assure both the maintenance of the structures of production and the standard of living of the ruling classes, the weight of the bureaucracy becomes oppressive. Feeling the consequences of popular discontent, the bureaucracy seeks to obtain a maximum of political autonomy, and to set itself up as a ruling class.

The key fact in the evolution of Western countries is that the capitalist system of production created a process of appropriating surplus value that in theory dispensed with the role of the bureaucracy as an intermediary. The young Marx based his vision of capitalism's destruction upon this meaning of the capitalist mode of production: the overthrow of capitalism would at the same time relegate the state to "the museum of history". The substitution of the private ("voluntary") appropriation of surplus value for state appropriation had already begun to undermine the principal function of the state. The working class, by altering the legal status of the owners of the means of production, and by transforming their private property into productive property, would transform itself into the collective user of the surplus value produced by itself through the process of industrial accumulation; and, it would thereby bring an end to surplus value itself, as the product of the exploitation of man by man.

But we know today that the historical fulfilment of this process has been postponed to a future time, because of the new qualitative and quantitative needs created by the liberation of the productive forces of heavy industry. We also know how state capitalism set itself up as the regulator of the whole economy in substituting itself for liberal capitalism. But that is another subject.

In any case, if we accept these premises for analyzing the internal evolution of socialist countries, we also observe that the conditions foreseen by the Marxist authors did not yet exist, and because of the existence of a more developed foreign capitalism, could never have existed. The primitive accumulation of capital required the reinforcement (not the withering away) of the state bureaucracy as an agent for the appropriation of surplus value — that is, it required external control exercised by the bureaucracy over economic mechanisms, and in particular over the private production of the peasantry. The political weight of the bureaucratic class was made that much stronger. For the first time in the history of European societies (if one leaves aside the Creto-Mycenaen era in which it seems that the Asiatic mode of production dominated), the bureaucracy found itself in the position of directly managing the economy.*

*Eliminating External Control
over the Mode of Industrial Production*

The realisation of the bureaucracy's objective condemned it to eventual death. As Eastern European societies were transformed from agrarian into

---

* Nevertheless - contrary to the theses of Milovan Djilas in *The New Class* — the essential part of the bureaucracy's power is extra-economic. Its control is first of all political control. Stalinist or Rakosist 'voluntarism' is a caricature of this.

industrial societies, the number of direct producers of surplus value (industrial and agricultural wage earners, and workers in productive services) increased accordingly. The appropriation of surplus value through external control became an obstacle to the internal growth of productive forces, and began to appear more and more as an anachronism.

It is from this point of view that one must understand the revival of "the market", the autonomous management of enterprises, and the decentralization of the planning apparatus. The autonomous management of enterprises on the scale of capitalist enterprises of the same kind makes it possible for the directors of these enterprises to escape fiscal control by means of self-investment and to establish direct, unmediated relations among themselves. It is a means of giving economic initiative to the directors of the enterprises and of taking it away from the centralized state bureaucracy. In a word, it isn't a question of eliminating the appropriation of surplus value, but of eliminating the external control over the mode of industrial production.

The technocratic stratum appeared at the head of this offensive. It constituted itself as the upper class of economic directors, who passed from a position as specialised employees of the state bureaucracy to becoming principally responsible for economic activity. This stratum developed as industry in the socialist countries grew and became diversified.

Among the financial techniques that began to come into use were accelerated amortization, self-financing, free disposition of saleable stock re-inserted into the balance sheets of assets and

Falling production graph hounds the director out of his office.

From Ludas matyi (Budapest), Oct. 30, 1969.

liabilities and free from taxation, and inter-enterprise loans. From this point of view, "economic reform" in the USSR, Czechoslovakia, and Hungary seems to have gone in the direction followed by European liberal capitalism in the nineteenth century, where political control over the producer classes gave way to economic control, and where the state itself was gradually reduced to the role of policeman. The partisans of Mao Tse-Tung, viewing these developments, speak of the "restoration of capitalism" in the USSR. But, in so doing, they reflect an archaic conception of a bureaucracy placed in conditions identical to those of the Stalinist bureaucracy of the first five-year plans. One may just as well maintain that "the free society of producers" that the First International inscribed on its flags is hardly conceivable without the exercise of intelligent initiative by individual enterprises.

Technocracy as Tied to the Uninterrupted Development of the Productive Forces

We cannot ignore the particular character of the technocratic stratum in socialist countries, where there is no private ownership of the means of production, and where such a stratum cannot expect to find support in perpetuating itself indefinitely. Nor can we ignore the fact that the liberation of the internal accumulative mechanisms of large-scale production tends increasingly to bring the majority of workers together in a concern for self-management. The maintenance and development of the privileges of the technocratic stratum are founded upon the uninterrupted development of the productive forces. Stagnation or regression brings an end to its power and influence. The technocracy does not prosper simply by virtue of its position. In this sense, its power is totally different from that of the state bureaucracy. The struggle between them that ensues is between a technocracy that bases its power on internal economic mechanisms — on the growth of the productive forces — and a bureaucracy installed in fossilized structures — using police control as a response to its incapacity to master the new economic processes. The echoes of this struggle have been heard in all post-Stalinist literature over the last ten years — from *Not by Bread Alone* to *Engineer Bakhirev.*

In restoring to the economy its guiding role in the development of new social and cultural relations, the technocracy reinforces the specific weight of the direct producers of social wealth. The technocracy has neither the means to buy its labour force — because it is not the owner of the means of production — nor any power to control work by force, since it does not control the police or judiciary. The struggle waged by Soviet technocrats, allied with liberal intellectuals, against such leftovers from the Stalin era as the "corrective labour camps" is symbolic. Stalin's concentration camps, like those of the Nazis, appear to them a caricature of relations of production that bureaucracy spontaneously led to: the negation of the natural effects of the economic dynamic, physical control substituted for "economic stimulants", the radical suppression of the requirements of the consumer, the voluntarism of the bureaucracy that became a law for the economy, and an economy geared towards prestige efforts upon the success of which the bureaucratic stratum could flatter itself.

31

The Qualitative Development of the Productive Forces

In this struggle, the technocracy today carries within it the future possibility of socialism, in which "the administration of things will replace the administration of men", without itself being socialist. I would like to recall again an important factor in this struggle: the technocracy, as a homogenous social group and as the sum of the particular interests of each technocrat (including cultural, scientific, and professional interests), finds its strength in the qualitative development of the productive forces. Preoccupation with such development is fundamentally foreign to the bureaucracy. The technocracy is first and foremost interested in the development of the most modern forms of technology (such as automation), in the continuous rise in the level of qualifications of the working class, and in the generalised development of scientific research. In this way, it tends to accelerate the process of the generalised formation of a class of worker-technicians. One might say that the process that brought about the formation of the Soviet technocratic class is the same that led to the constitution of a "new working class", technically qualified and deeply integrated into the process of production.

The Development of the Technocracy Creates a "New Working Class"

One of Lenin's most dramatic errors (in company with Trotsky and Stalin) was not seeing the consequences that the introduction of the assembly line would have upon the political and social consciousness of Soviet workers. The resulting technological alienation would only strengthen the hold of the bureaucracy upon a working class which would remain a minority. On the other hand, the third industrial revolution that the Soviet technocrats are working feverishly to bring about favours an awakening of consciousness on the part of the working masses and a desire to control the management of the economy. Within Socialist countries, during the present period, the restoration of the rights of the consumer — that is, of the producer outside of the sphere of production — will have similar effects on the development of social self-management.

The formation of the technocracy in the Soviet Union and in the People's Democracies takes place within legal relations of production identical to those in which the bureaucratic stratum flowered: relations of production of the "state capitalist" variety. The exploitation of man by man has not been abolished: the state appropriates from labour a profit going far beyond the "general expenses of society". Social equality is very far from being established; there still exists the relation of dominator to dominated and of rulers to ruled; and the accumulation of capital remains the motor of the economy's development. The fact that the Twenty-Second Congress characterised the Soviet State as "the State of the Entire People" (an expression of Lassalle's that Marx considered an expression of "state capitalism") proves furthermore that the Soviet theoreticians are more conscious of this fact than is generally believed.

The Two Phases of State Capitalism

However, state capitalism in the bureaucratic phase

differs profoundly from state capitalism in the technocratic phase. In state capitalism of the first phase, the 1924-1955 period in the USSR and, roughly, from 1947 to 1955 in the People's Democracies, the bureaucracy had no other economic function than to apportion among the vital sectors of heavy industry and the civilian and military bureaucracy the appropriations taken from the mass of the population, and principally from the mass of private producers in the country and small towns. The bureaucracy was occupied with the organisation of scarcity.

The economic management of state capitalism in the present phase must be described in completely different terms: private producers have almost completely disappeared, and the increasing majority of salaried, urban workers has created large masses of modern consumers, requiring a qualitative diversification of products distributed. Furthermore, the relative scarcity of the postwar years encouraged considerable private savings for which people today are seeking an outlet not in capital investment (which is removed from individual capitalist initiative) but in consumer goods. The development of the automobile industry in the USSR and the People's Democracies proves that this demand has been stronger than the will of the politicians and the planners.

One might regret, however, that the model of consumption found in Eastern countries resembles so much the model developed in capitalist countries — one which subordinates the realisation of social needs to the realisation of individual ones. This is one of the most serious consequences of the bureaucracy's impotence in organizing an "abundant" society: poverty, inconvenience, and the defective functioning of collective equipment all render inevitable the search for comfort at an individual level, just as the maintenance of official salaries at a rate inferior to economic growth is responsible for wide-spread moonlighting and camouflaged forms of adding to one's income.

This tendency imposes on the economies of Eastern countries a double task: to satisfy the individual demand that has already appeared and to forestall the growth of this tendency through a qualitative improvement in collective equipment.

Technocratic state capitalism must respond to the inevitable need for industrial diversification, to the need for the multiplication of service jobs and for better qualified personnel to fill them. It must respond to the need for a generalised development of pure and applied scientific research that no longer concentrates on certain sectors considered essential by the bureaucracy.

It cannot avoid establishing competition among enterprises in order to watch over the profitability of investments — a rich society whose needs are well-developed can less afford waste than a poor society. It must guard against the over-development (however inevitable) of certain sectors, and must seek the maximum utilization of reserves. In a word, state capitalism in the second phase can no longer count on any extra-economic control. This is the profound significance of the "goulash social-ism" that the peasant Khrushchev promised, but whose precise costs — far different in nature than a robust Muzhik soup — were left to the industrialist

Kosygin to assess. The autonomy of enterprises, the criterion of profitability, the actual costs of production, and the growing demand of a technically and culturally maturing working class cause the rigid framework of bureaucratic planning to burst, multiply the centres of decision-making, and engender in Soviet and Eastern European society polarities that contest these decisions.

The industrial, scientific or technical technocracy, conscious of these processes, finds its present strength and succeeds in winning over the old bureaucracy only because it appears as the representative of the desires and needs of "the whole society".

The danger lies in just this fact. For the bureaucracy at first played a positive role in relation to the needs of an agrarian society moving towards industrialization, only to become an obstacle to its development later on. In going back to 1936-1937 to find the beginning of "the negative period of the cult of personality", Soviet theoreticians and rulers admit explicitly that since that period the phase of bureaucratic state capitalism had ceased to be necessary.(The new Soviet constitution of 1936 was, moreover, the theoretical recognition of this fact.) Unfortunately, the bureaucracy had been developing all through this period without any opposition. Neither the workers' opposition, broken in 1938 when the unions were chastened, nor the purged Bolshevik Old Guard, nor the terrorized intellectuals were in a position to express at that time the objective aspirations of Soviet society. One cannot consider as positive this unnecessary prolongation of the bureaucratic phase, even taking into account the danger of world war; for the Soviet Union was very poorly prepared for the World War by the Stalinist bureaucracy — politically, diplomatically, and militarily.

The Dangers of the Uncontrolled Exercise of Technocratic Power

The dangers of the uncontrolled exercise of technocratic power aren't the same as those that flow from an all-powerful bureaucracy. But those dangers are no less real, nor are they less of a constraint upon the development of the socialist process. The bureaucracy is voluntarist, while the technocracy is empiricist. The technocracy has the tendency to follow the "spontaneous" currents in the economy, currents that international commerce orient more in certain directions than others. And the concern with short-term profit leads it to renounce with ease objectives judged beyond reach.

Recognizing the Working Class, but subordinating It.

The technocracy's orientation toward establishing new social relations is ambiguous: on one hand, it knows that in a modern industrial system requiring qualified personnel, one can no longer do without the support of the working class. The introduction of new technology requires the integration of workers by contract. Neo-capitalist Western society has come to recognize the importance of that integration. It is all the more important in a society where "socialism" remains the governing ideology and goal, and in which the private ownership of the means of production does not set up a legal barrier between the worker and the enterprise. The technocracy is thus led to seek the "participation" of the workers in the functioning of the enterprise. We should not forget that the bureaucracy, the reflection of a state which proclaims itself a workers' state, freely considered itself as the reflection of the workers themselves and was so much the more determined to refuse them the right to speak, in the name of the bureaucracy's "representative" status. The technocracy does not share this charismatic power. It sees itself as different from the working class which it is thus constrained to *recognize* as a partner in the realization of economic objectives.

On the other hand, the technocracy has the tendency to transform this recognition into subordination: it will accept a better distribution of salaries, multiply individual incentives, abandon to workers the management of the collective social part of the salary — the social services of the enterprise — but in the name of its special competence, it will refuse the workers access to economic management itself. It wants sole decision-making power over investments, market retail prices, and production orientation. In order to secure this power, the technocracy of the socialist countries, just like its Western counterparts, will have the tendency to redirect the workers' demand for managerial power toward the satisfaction of their consumer needs — needs that it holds the power to orient.

In the most evolved Western societies, these relations already exist in a popular mode: they come under the name of "collective bargaining". But Western technocracy (European or American) is protected by capitalist relations of production and appears officially as the management of the capitalist class. That fact causes the paradoxical development within the working class of a conflicting set of feelings about these relations that encourages it to go beyond the simple higher wage demand. The technocracy in socialist countries can take refuge behind "the collective ownership of the means of production" and appear as the manager of the property of "all the people". This gives it an "objective" character that Western technocracy has difficulty in imposing.

4

"Reform": Retrospect and Prospects

Socialist countries have not escaped from the law of unequal regional development any more than capitalist countries. As long as there was a situation of general scarcity and as long as the centralised bureaucracy used extra-economic controls as a means of collecting taxes, this gap between more and less developed regions remained small or was passively accepted. The style of life of the Muslim regions of the Soviet East or that of the primitive mountain communities of the Caucasus were so different from that of the urban centres that no comparison could be made.

The creation by the bureaucracy of a unique market of consumers, the homogenisation of social classes, the administrative uniformity inherent in the whole bureaucratic apparatus, and the transplantation of entire populations to production sites chosen by the authorities have fundamentally changed this situation. Because the ruling bureaucratic stratum draws its power from the total appropriation of surplus value, it imposes a relative homogenisation of living conditions and style of life. In the meantime, the artificial character of general distribution has only masked the unequal development without correcting it.

Moreover, the quantitative character of production has allowed the old industrial regions to age and fossilise without the leaders of these regions noticing this fact. The supremacy of political power over the economy has thus allowed zones of technical backwardness to develop whose level of revenue is only maintained through subsidies. Besides, bureaucratic decisions have created costly enterprises without consideration of retail prices. There are the notorious "political factories", destined to transform the consciousness of the peasant masses, to pull them away from the agrarian mode of life and thus attach them to "socialism".

Social Difficulties of Economic Reconversion

The reconversion away from this past is an absolute necessity in order to permit the passage of the economy of countries with socialist structures to a qualitatively superior level. But the reconversion creates important social contradictions.

"Administrative socialism" assured to the working classes a dull security: salaries were miserable, but jobs were assured. Consumer goods were rare, expensive, and of mediocre quality, but work was most of the time not very tiring. The material handled by the workers was antiquated, but they worked routinely with it as they had learned to do ten or twenty years before. The absence of any renovation of equipment or techniques excused workers and technicians from the effort of

41

permanent readaptation which the modification of techniques entails. Paradoxically, the socialist bureaucracy, after having exalted constructive effort in its ascendant phase, after having distributed medals to the "Stakhanovists" and "Oudarniks", had come to the point of letting laziness and an "I don't give a damn" attitude corrode all the gears of production. The economic reform upsets all these habits; its brutal application is causing veritable social crises. In certain cases, it throws out of the productive circuit elements that cannot adapt to the changes; in others, it also throws out those who have not had the time to adapt. Because it sometimes affects not only entire enterprises but whole regions and economic sectors, it provokes serious ruptures in the equilibrium among regions. The experience of developed capitalist countries has demonstrated that the rigorous application of the laws of economic competition can in time destroy the very seeds of reconversion in a region undergoing structural crisis.

The Bureaucracy Rediscovers Its Political Base

When the "political factories" that were opened during the last ten years in Yugoslavian Bosnia and in Slovakia begin to close by the dozens, the managers and the young of these areas will experience the fate of older workers. The whole region will risk falling back into the state of underdevelopment from which it had only — through state subsidies — superficially emerged. There is a real possibility that barely extinguished national passions will reawaken, inflamed by this state of affairs.

42

"You are fit for work, comrade deputy manager, but you are certainly not fit for your job."
From Hospodarske noviny (Prague), Oct. 6, 1967

"Poujadist" reactions* on the part of the old working class, with its inadequate education, its inability to readapt, "nationalist" reactions of marginal regions that falsely believed they were on the road to industrialization — these are some of the elements that give the old bureaucratic stratum a mass base that it has not enjoyed for many years. One has seen Hungarian workers longing for the times of Rakosi, Serbian workers rallying to the Rankovitch banner, and Novotny and his followers have found among a part of the Czech working class a base that has permitted them to hold out for long months against the "technocrat offensive."

A more intensive analysis permits us also to perceive contradictions that are dependent upon those mentioned above but even more significant: the first was revealed when the economic reform brought to light an informal network of communication and exchange that had grown up within the inequality tolerated under the apparent uniformity of bureaucratic production. This network brought with it numerous opportunities for illegal and semi-legal economic activity. One example is the Kolkhoz peasants near large urban markets who, because of the complex distribution mechanism for agricultural products, found ways of realizing, thanks to the free market, more than sixty to seventy percent of their total revenue on their private plots — to the detriment of the Kolkhoz. Another is the extraordinary prolifera-

* Poujade is a French political leader who defends the autonomy and independence of underdeveloped French regions on behalf of a peasant and petit-bourgeois constituency. [Ed.]

tion of small dealers on the black market; still others are the systematic thefts in the factories, and the clandestine manufacture of scarce consumer goods. All these "little interests" weigh against the reform.

The "Pseudo-Equality" of the New Social Differentiations

The second and even graver contradiction, because it upsets the basis for collective consciousness, is the apparent extension of social inequalities engendered by economic reform. The privileges of the bureaucratic stratum were hidden beneath its status as a servant of the State, which protects it from public attention. In the beginning, these privileges were limited to a narrow layer of the population, living above and outside the daily life of the masses. Below this layer, small-time profiteers of the bureaucracy were obliged to conceal their gains. They continually risked discovery from an unexpected change in management that might bring to light their illegal practices, with the usual ugly consequences. Most of the population thus lived in a relatively egalitarian climate, an equality based upon equal poverty to be sure, but poverty is better tolerated when it is general.

Economic reform, in restoring to work the norms of effective social labour, does away with this dull egalitarianism. It diminishes the revenue of certain less productive industrial sectors and raises that of others. The disparity of revenue, along with the new opportunities given higher incomes to buy consumer goods heretofore considered luxuries, becomes a visible phenomenon in daily life. It is more difficult not to have a car

45

when one's neighbour has one; it is more difficult than when cars were reserved for managers of the regime who only used them when escorted by motorcycle police .... The Pobeda of one's neighbour is less tolerable than the Mercedes of the Party secretary or of the Trust director.

Condemned to irrelevance by economic evolution, the old bureaucratic stratum is thus finding within the inheritance of its own social system a new means to survival:

—It ties its own fate to that of elements of the population who found the means to live well by selling their illegal or semi-legal services, an exchange which the bureaucracy had tolerated as an escape valve but which the reform tends to eliminate.

—It can appeal to the socialist consciousness latent in the population against the deepening process of social differentiation.

—It can find a mass base in underdeveloped or artifically developed regions, as well as in regions that are declining because of antiquated techniques.

—It can give singular expression to the fears of the most backward sectors — the oldest but most numerous — of the working class, threatened by job and status insecurity.

It would thus be naive to believe that "objective necessities" will be sufficient in themselves to liquidate rapidly the bureaucratic system. On the contrary, the system finds a new political vigour precisely in the struggle waged against it and in the social consequences of the attempt to eliminate its own inheritance. Its new strength is analogous to that manifested elsewhere and in other conditions by reactionary groups on the defensive: one need only think of the depth of resistance of the old labour force of archaic capitalist enterprises in France when they rallied to Poujade, or the difficulties encountered by American neo-capitalism in imposing political structures adapted to the level of the productive forces of the largest capitalist country.

But at the same time, "economic reform" is no longer the occasion of academic jousts or of devious conflicts within the State apparatus, but is becoming an open political conflict. The "economic reformers" of the USSR did not originally seek an open conflict with the reigning bureaucracy. They participated to a certain extent in the bureaucratic process; they belonged to the same "new elite" that emerged from the revolutionary process, and their evolution is a result of the differentiation of functions within the bureaucracy. This leads them to desire structural change rather than to "seize power". In this respect, the socialist technocrats strongly resemble their capitalist counterparts who disdain, by their very nature, any thought of assuming political responsibility for the changes that they wish to make, and who spend their lives searching for charismatic leaders, from de Gaulle to Kennedy, who will impose upon the politicians and the conservative capitalist elements the changes which they deem necessary.

Another reason for fearing an open conflict with the bureaucracy is the technocracy's fear of social and economic disruption. Caring little for public discussion of the consequences of the reforms, jealous of its directorial functions, it would prefer, if possible, to "convince" the ruling apparatus of its good intentions, and to maintain the hierarchical structures in which it exercises its power, structures which sharp political battle might topple.

The Soviet Union still seems to be in the stage of conflict in which the antagonism between the old ruling group and the new one has not come out into the open. The weak state of "public opinion". the conformity of the press, the influence of the army, which arbitrates in the name of national defence, all mitigate against open conflict. But, perhaps the most important factor is the extraordinary solidarity that the sense of responsibility for world empire gives to the ruling groups. Imperial consciousness has always succeeded in smoothing over the sharpest social contradictions, as long as the Empire remains intact.

Imperial Consciousness as a Factor
in The Reduction of Internal Conflicts

But things are not, nor can they be the same in the People's Democracies of Eastern Europe. Several factors play a role in accelerating conflict there, so that it is in Eastern Europe, and not in the Soviet Union, that the evolution of societies with a socialist structure will take the most explosive forms.

1. The People's Democracies are today largely open to Western tourism and commerce, and thus are confronted (more than the USSR) with the need for *qualitative* changes in the organization of production. The passage from a massified, quantitative economy that assures everyone their elementary needs, but limits the satisfaction of these needs to the amelioration of the standard of living, to a diversified, qualitative economy that

permits choices, has become a demand of the masses in Prague, Budapest, Belgrade, and Bucharest.

2. The Russian Bureaucracy, or as Lenin would say, the "Great Russian" bureaucracy, is a national bureaucracy. The bureaucracy of other Eastern countries appears more often than not as the executive of the wishes of the Russian bureaucracy. The tendencies toward "decentralization" and toward the autonomy of industrial management has a peculiar character there — this internal autonomy will lead in time to an external national autonomy.

The return to "economic rationality", the re-establishment of market mechanisms, the diversification of production, all appear as different ways of correcting the situation of political dependence through indirect economic means, and at the same time gaining some autonomy for economic decision-making.

In this regard, the struggle of the technocracy tends in the People's Democracies to become a national struggle: the reform not only calls into question local bureaucratic power, but it also undermines the relations of political and economic domination established between the USSR and the small European countries belonging to the "socialist camp". The plans for economic reform in both Rumania and Czechoslovakia are directly at odds with the structure of Comecon, which authorizes relations among socialist states only at the level of central ministries.

The above explains more clearly the ambiguous relations between the Soviet technocracy and the

Eastern European technocrats. In certain ways the Soviet technocrats wish — or at least wished in the beginning — to see the People's Democracies *experiment* with models of economic reform. Both the objective technological and economic conditions (cultural and technical level on the average more advanced, industrial traditions more widespread, markets both more homogenous and less extended, more advanced national integration, nearness to Western Europe) and the political conditions (weakness of the national bureaucratic class) allowed the European People's Democracies to move through the *stages* upon which the Soviet reformers could then build. The interest shown by Soviet economists in the Yugoslav economic reform, the encouragement of Kosygin himself for the Czech reformers, notably for Ota Sik, are incontestable proof of this.

But the consequences of economic reform in the People's Democracies for relations in the socialist camp were not slow in appearing. The first conflict with the Ceausescu government in Rumania concerned the level of autonomy of Rumanian industrial production and the nature of its trade with the West. The economic reform introduced in Hungary led it to multiply its inter-enterprise relations, not only with socialist countries such as Yugoslavia and Czechoslovakia, but with Austria, and the German Democratic Republic. The Czech reformers never hid the fact that managerial autonomy also signified for them liberation for their international activities. The dismantling of the bureaucratic system of national planning brought with it the dismantling not only of the heavy and unreal Comecon apparatus, but also that of the bilateral systems preferentially tying each of the People's Democracies to the Soviet Union. And the attempts made by the reformers to give Comecon another status and to create within it a sort of little Common Market of Danubian countries were not received any better by Soviet planners than were the overtures to the West made by Bucharest, Prague and Budapest.

In comparing Comecon with the Common Market, we in Western Europe forget too easily that Comecon more closely resembles as association of the diverse Common Market countries taken together with the United States of America.

To this disproportion among "equal partners" in Comecon is added the backwardness of the Soviet economy which, with the exception of certain privileged sectors (notably in military production) finds itself incapable of putting into play the mechanisms of "structural" domination by which the USA controls certain capitalist economies (Great Britain, Canada, Italy, and to a certain degree, Germany, France and Japan). These would include the ownership of patents, selective investments, organic integration of peak industries into large trusts, etc. The Soviet empire, from the point of view of its methods of economic domination, rests very often on the level of classical colonialism, especially with regard to the appropriation of raw materials.

Soviet technocrats, no matter how good their intentions with regard to reforms in the People's Democracies, can't go beyond a certain threshold of "liberalism" — that which would allow the economy of Central Europe to break out of the

Soviet economic orbit. This will remain the case as long as the Soviet Union does not have the means to replace political and military forms of domination with economic ones. This stage will not be possible until the Soviet Union itself achieves its own economic reform, if it can do so. In the meantime, the People's Democracies are expected to "mark time".

One should not even exclude the possibility that the USSR might attain a level of economic and political liberalization which it would deny its satellites. After all, neither "liberal" Great Britain of the nineteenth century, nor Republican France exported their own interior models to their colonies or their zones of influence.

But this contradiction between the rhythm of passage from the bureaucratic to the technocratic phase in the USSR and the rhythm she is willing to accept in the People's Democracies is full of consequences:

1. First, in the Soviet Union itself: the limits that "the imperial consciousness" imposes upon technocratic reformers in the USSR in their fight with the old bureaucracy reinforces the contradiction. It cuts them off from the non-technocratic intelligentsia, and from the students who welcome the audacity of the Eastern European Communists as worthy examples to imitate, being less receptive than their elders to Russian nationalism.

These limits oblige the technocrats to accept the weight of external controls: traditional military force, unusable in a world war, but playing a necessary "gendarme" role in the Empire along with the "ideological edicts" of the bureaucracy. An example of the latter is the unfolding of the "anti-Zionist" wave in Poland, and the anti-Semitic propaganda used almost continuously against the Czech and Rumanian reformers, that doesn't stop at the borders of the USSR. (The father of the Russian economic reform, Liberman, is "more Jewish" than Ota Sik.)

The "imperial" situation of the Soviet Union as a consequence acts as a brake upon the passage from the bureaucratic to the technocratic phase, just as, *mutatis mutandis,* the arrival of neo-capitalism in France and Great Britain was slowed down by ten or fifteen years by the imperial character of French and English capitalism. Kosygin clearly does not have the audacity of de Gaulle, who understood that the reformation of old French capitalism depended upon "auctioning off the empire".

2. The limits upon economic reform brought about by the USSR's imperial position affect the character of the struggle in the People's Democracies between the technocracy and the bureaucracy. They give this struggle an open character and force the technocracy to seek popular support — to build a mass base that, in turn, transforms the nature of the passage from bureaucratic to technocratic control.

But this transformation can certainly take different (and less pronounced) forms. In Rumania, for instance, the modern technocracy that has captured the leadership of the Party and the State has not fundamentally modified social and political relations. The "liberalization" of economic life is scarcely perceptible except to the new generation of administrators, high-level technicians, and scientific executives who control the "islands of modernity" in a country that for the most part is still backward. These islands are found in the most recently developed sectors of Rumanian industry — for instance, petro-chemicals. National feeling, reinforced by old animosities toward Slavic and Russian peoples, is enough for the moment to assure the reformist regime the popular support it needs to resist Rumania's powerful neighbour.

But the example of Yugoslavia demonstrates that in the long run national feeling is not enough. The Yugoslavian leaders, who in 1945 proclaimed themselves "the best Stalinists in the Balkans" have subsequently formally instituted worker and social self-management, which, even if limited in practice, has allowed for fairly extensive free discussion and criticism. They have, for instance, tolerated the existence in such journals as *Praxis* of veritable poles of intellectual contention. This process will probably occur in Rumania too.

But the transformation is naturally even more rapid in countries that are more industrialized, such as Hungary and above all, Czechoslovakia. Here, the struggle for "the economic reform" cannot avoid becoming a social and political struggle of great amplitude. The *de facto* liquidation of a large part of the Stalinist bureaucracy in Hungary, its incredible loss of prestige in Czechoslovakia, leads it inevitably to seek the direct support of the Russians, and their direct or indirect intervention in blocking reform. This can be seen very clearly in the actions of the people around Novotny. The bureaucracy also tends to assure itself a direct political base in that part of the population,

"Mrs. Mullerova, you'll testify, won't you, that we've all been progressives!"

From Dikobraz (Prague), June 20, 1968.

especially among workers, who might fear the consequences of the reform. But by the same token, the "reformers" are obliged to seek not simply popular consensus, but the true support of the masses, support that can extend to active political struggles.

It is here that the technocracy, by nature cautious about political action, finds itself obliged to seek support among new strata of the population — among workers and technicians in advanced industries, high school and college youth, and among intellectuals. Henceforth, the processes underway in Czechoslovakia will go beyond the conflict between the bureaucracy and technocracy. The extensive questioning of authoritarian socialism that is proceeding there has spilled over the confines set by economic reform, and has begun to raise the problem of social self-management. One can see, for example, the convergence between the analyses made by Ota Sik's people and those made in France by Charles Bettleheim. For these two Marxist economists, socialist society has not yet reached the stage of development of which Marx dreamed where it is possible to generalize the process of social autonomy but the socialist management of large autonomous and coordinated units already holds within it the possibility of such a future.

In proclaiming that *"social self-management must be achieved at the level of the real socialization of the process of production"*, Ota Sik indicated what roads could lead to a society not entirely socialist—i.e., completely self-managed — but that would allow for large sectors of concrete self-management in areas where activity specifically conditions the future of the country — precisely those areas where the working class has both the desire and the ability to exercise self-management.

From this point of view, the process of self-management envisaged by Czech reformers goes beyond the legally larger framework of Yugoslav self-management. Yugoslavia, which has decreed the self-management of all industrial enterprises, whether service or commercial enterprises, has at the same time limited the possiblity for workers' councils to coordinate their activities at the level of branches or trusts. This enlargement, envisaged between 1959 and 1962, was bitterly fought by the Yugoslav bureaucracy, which saw in it the threat of "dual power".

It is true that this power given to the workers' councils would essentially have affirmed the authority of the largest and most modern enterprises, and would have in some manner given these sectors hegemony over less advanced sectors of production. But this situation would at the same time have reactivated the life of unions in the economically weaker sectors.

The possiblity of seeing temporary antagonisms between sectors of the working class expressed in terms of real social conflicts — as has already happened between various federal republics — would perhaps require a verbal retreat from the conception of a socialism free from social contradictions. But it would surely be a real advance toward a democratic and self-determined socialism, in which the masses participate actively in political life, instead of abandoning their fate to the obscure manoeuvres of "ruling elites".

The beginnings of political activity along the most advanced sectors of the Czechoslovakian working class — those that prefer the risks of real self-management to the illusory security of bureaucratic planning — is far healthier in nature and furnishes much more cause for hope than the mysteries that surround decision-making in the Kremlin. Theoretical research on the roads to socialism must now emerge from the academic arena and "descend into the street".

Because they were forced to seek public support to resist pressure from the Russians, the Czech technocracy consciously or unconsciously opened the way to a practical — active — experience of socialist democracy. Economic reform is tending to become social reform. The actors are no longer the directors and high administrative functionaries, but rather the most dynamic forces of Czech society. The passage from the bureaucratic to the technocratic phase, because it is happening as open political conflict, is unleashing a new process that undermines the possibility of a prolonged hegemony for the technocracy, and opens the opportunity of social self-management.

Such is the tremendous historial importance of the changes now occuring in Eastern European countries. They seem to prefigure those that will happen sooner or later in the Soviet Union. Of course, the final realization of these possiblities also depends upon the possiblities of socialist revolution in Western Europe, but that is another subject.

5

After the Soviet Intervention in Czechoslovakia

The Soviet occupation of Czechoslovakia coincided with the period of the re-birth of a mass revolutionary movement in the capitalist countries of Western Europe : I might cite first of all the main movement in France; the increasingly acute social and political crisis in Italy; the continual strengthening of the revolutionary movement in Spain; the transformation of the Basque nationalist and separatist movement into a socialist revolutionary movement; the appearance in the Federal Republic of West Germany of a powerful extra-parliamentary opposition involving not only the majority of students but also large factions of the social democratic trade union movement. The emergence of a new socialist and revolutionary left in Germany has already helped to modify the policies of West German diplomacy, to stem the development towards the right of the social-democracy, and to influence the liberal movement in Germany to veer towards the left. And finally, there was the radicalisation of an important section of the trade unions in Great Britain, especially in the most advanced industries. For the first time since 1947, Western Europe witnessed the re-birth of a dynamic socialist movement capable of revealing concrete possibilities of a transition to socialism in several of the advanced capitalist countries. Western Europe, while tolerating less and less readily the economic and political domination of American capitalism, was becoming aware of the failure of various neo-capitalist solutions propounded by various bourgeois and social democratic coalition governments, and this was particularly true of the younger people in all those countries.

This development taking place in western Europe was principally due to internal structural characteristics of the various countries involved, but it was also conditioned by the lessening of the danger of war, including the cold war, in Europe; by the progressive liberalisation of several East European countries, particularly Hungary and later on Czechoslovakia; and by the apparent beginning of the transformation of the Soviet military bloc into a more flexible form of alliance; and finally, by the growing strength within the international communist movement of so-called polycentrist tendencies such as those championed by the Italian communists since 1956. This was particularly true in countries with a catholic tradition where Catholic peasants and workers and large elements of the clergy are attracted to socialism but want it to be based on broad democratic procedures and ideological pluralism. This is also true of the new class of technologists and of the mass of young people, peasants and workers as well as priests.

The various progressive developments in Eastern Europe, already referred to, weakened traditional anti-communism in the West and encouraged protests against American crimes in Vietnam, the Dominican Republic and elsewhere. The overthrow of Novotny and his clique in Czechoslovakia, the immense popular support in Czechoslovakia for the new communist party membership, the proof that socialism is not only compatible with democracy, but is actually helped by democracy in getting rid of its own inner weaknesses, have all played an important part in the development of revolutionary socialism in Western Europe. As in 1848, the revolutionary tide was out to smash conservatism wherever it might exist.

The Soviet intervention in Czechoslovakia dealt a heavy blow to the hope that socialism and liberty could be reconciled in the countries of Eastern Europe. The negative consequence of the Soviet intervention in Czechoslovakia for the socialist movement throughout the world and especially in western Europe can be summarised as follows.

First, the experiment conducted in Czechoslovakia, the only country among the people's democracies with a tradition both of bourgeois democracy and of a revolutionary working-class movement, the only one whose option for socialism had been achieved by the decision of an electoral majority, was a model of absolutely decisive importance for Western Europe. We believe that the development of socialism in Czechoslovakia, which had been temporarily diverted by the cold war and the character of the centralised bureaucracy which had been imposed on Czechoslovakia by the Stalinists, was going to resume its original course. The theoretical discussions and practical steps undertaken by Czechoslovak communists were felt to be of profound interest to western socialism. Not everyone agreed with or approved of all the theories which were canvassed in Czechoslovakia, but, for the first time, an experiment in the building of socialism was of immediate concern to us and could serve us as a point of reference.

Secondly, the Soviet action in this crisis has re-awakened all the fears and spectres of the cold war.

None of the arguments advanced by the U.S.S.R. in defence of its intervention, has met with the slightest sympathy. The masses in Western Europe saw Soviet socialism as the mask of an imperialist power, with only its own state interests at heart, but the confusion which has existed for thirty years between the Soviet Union and socialism, still persists, and the Soviet action meant that the mass of the people of Western Europe felt repelled by socialism.

Thirdly, the theoretical justifications advanced by the Soviet Union did us perhaps more harm than the action itself. By adopting the view, contrary to the theory of the national question as developed by Lenin, (and even by Stalin) that the Soviet Union was entitled to intervene, even by force, in the internal affairs of any socialist country, because it alone could decide what was good socialism and was not, the Soviet Union have seriously jeopardised the future of all socialist forces in the world. In France we may well ask ourselves whether, had the French communist party been in power, they would be held subject to the same dictum? If so, the Soviet action in Czechoslovakia would have been rubber stamped. Add to this the virulent attacks in *Pravda* and other Soviet newspapers against the French revolution in May 1968. Many people genuinely dedicated to the cause of socialism felt that the presence of the communist party in the government, in France that is, might automatically lead to the recognition of the Soviet Union's self-proclaimed right to armed intervention, and the step from this to a total refusal to co-operate with the French Communist Party was only a small one, and many people took it.

Fourthly, the Soviet intervention was based essentially on the concept of zones of influence, that is to say, it had the same basis as American imperialism in Vietnam, Brazil, Greece, and tomorrow who knows where? It has reinforced the feeling that the world is irrevocably divided. The countries of Western Europe, most of which are in the American sphere of influence, thus felt that any attempt to disengage themselves from the United States was bound to fail, and that they were condemned to go on suffering United States' domination. Thus a new weapon was handed on a plate to reactionary bourgeois and army circles.

Finally, there are grounds for fearing that other aggressive actions both inside and outside the orbit of the Soviet Union, may follow. It may be Rumania, Yugoslavia, Albania — any socialist country whose notion of socialism does not correspond to the Soviet one. A new wave of political terror may sweep the Soviet Union. After the revelations of the Twentieth Congress this would make all progressive forces throughout the world, with the small exception of those who need Soviet military and economic aid, (and by that token are clients rather than allies of the U.S.S.R.) renounce political solidarity with the U.S.S.R. In the face of the danger of the revival of the cold war this would inevitably reinforce conservative and authoritarian tendencies. I will conclude by saying that all Greek democrats are unanimous in saying that the Soviet intervention, by demoralising the left and scaring off the centre has done more to consolidate the fascist regime of the colonels of Greece than has the State Department. It may be feared that this is only an example which will be followed elsewhere.